Dear ANNIKA, June, 2018

Best wishes for exciting and fulfilling adventures as you travel around the world...

I Love you very much.

Love,
DAD

GLOBAL POETRY ANTHOLOGY

Global Poetry Anthology

2017

Montreal International Poetry Prize

EDITED BY

Kim Addonizio, David Dabydeen, Vona Groarke,
Susan Nalugwa Kiguli, Arvind Krishna Mehrotra,
Pascale Petit, Talya Rubin, Carmine Starnino,
Mark Tredinnick, Joseph Akawu Ushie

THE POETRY IMPRINT AT VÉHICULE PRESS

SIGNAL EDITIONS EDITOR: CARMINE STARNINO

Cover design: David Drummond
Set in Minion and MrsEaves by Simon Garamond
Printed by Marquis Book Printing Inc.

Copyright © The authors 2017
All rights reserved.

Dépôt légal, Library and Archives Canada and the
Bibliothèque national du Québec, fourth trimester 2017.

Montreal International Poetry Prize
www.montrealprize.com

Published by Véhicule Press, Montréal, Québec, Canada
www.vehiculepress.com

Distribution in Canada by LitDistCo
www.litdistco.ca

Distribution in the U.S. by Independent Publishers Group
www.ipgbook.com

Printed in Canada on FSC® certified paper.

Contents

PREFACE 7
ACKNOWLEDGEMENTS 8

Afternoons in and out of Paradise | Julie Watts 11
The Art Gallery | Chad Campbell 13
An Attitude of Waiters | Christopher (Kit) Kelen 15
Aubade | Mary B Moore 16
Blanksicle | Dominique Bernier-Cormier 17
Blue Curtains | Anthony Lawrence 18
Boa Gravida | Danielle Boodoo-Fortuné 20
Caesura | Erin Rodoni 21
Carnivores, The | Linda Rogers 22
Civil War At Parliament Hill Playground | James Greene 23
Degrees | Maithreyi Karnoor 24
Esos Huesos (Them Bones) | Lawrence Kessenich 25
Father Shouldn't Cry, A | Marsha Barber 27
Goya's Missing Skull | Barbara Hobbie 29
Guadalcanal | B. R. Dionysius 31
Here in White Swan | Allen Braden 33
Homestead | Elizabet Stevens 35
How a Typo Changed the World | Ann Gamsa 36
I Am Not Born... | Jnanama Ishaya 38
Kaieteur Falls (Potaro River, Guyana) | Fawzia Muradali Kane 40
My Ill-Omened, Mid-Life, First and Last,
Southern Wedding | Lauren Williams 42
Ode to My Period | Kate Rogers 44
Odile, The Black Swan | Una McDonnell 46
Old Blue Suitcase | Chloe Sparks 47
On the Other Side Of An Hour | Amber McMillan 48
Overture | Karey Willan 49
Return of the Spider Mother | David Mark Williams 51
San Vigilio de Marebe | Richard James 52

Seasonal Affective Disorder | Catriona Wright 54
Sewing | Bruce Meyer 56
Snow Crabs | Bruce Meyer 57
Soldiers | S. K. Kelen 58
Song from Cadiz | Zoe VanGunten 60
Song of the Water Lilies | Abigail Wieser 61
Story of Us, The | Anna Murchison 63
Stranded Conch, Alabama Coast | Peter Norman 65
Syzygy (Scrabble with Ivy) | Felicity Plunkett 67
The Wall Said | Derek Sugamosto 68
The Ways | Marjorie Main 70
They are Drawn Here In the Springtime | Bruce Van Noy 71
Thieves Have Gone , The | Christopher (Kit) Kelen 72
Time White Lightning Busted Out, The | Cynthia Hughes 74
Tranquil | Bryan Walpert 75
Twenty-two Days Before the First One Hundred Days | Rebecca Gayle Howell 76
Walk Along the Berlin Wall | Aimee Mackovic 78
When My Father Met Jesus | Cynthia Hughes 80
Wild Horses | J. P. Grasser 81
Windchime Meadows—Spring | Ashley Chan 82
You Have to Love Them Enough to Let Them be Wild | Kathleen McCracken 84
25 November 2016 | Margarita Serafimova 86

NOTES ON CONTRIBUTORS 89
NOTES ON EDITORS 99
AUTHOR INDEX 101

Preface

Greetings to the fourth edition of the *Global Poetry Anthology*. Once again, we are happy to present a truly international effort as our editors, hailing from Australia, Guyana, Ireland, Nigeria, Uganda, the UK, the US and, of course, from Canada, worked for several intensive weeks during the summer of 2017 to select the poems found herein. The result is a cosmopolitan cross-section of contemporary concerns, with poems about relationships, sex, death, conflict, war, faith, memory, nature and ecological threats. A perusal of this volume will carry you from inward journeys to Sacramento and on to Macon, Georgia in the USA, then on to San Vigilio de Marebe in Italy, to Cadiz in Spain, and onward for a walk along the Berlin Wall. We are proud to present yet another compelling collection of global poetry from a wide variety of poets, both accomplished and emerging.

For those unfamiliar with the Global Poetry Series, this anthology is the product of the 2017 Montreal International Poetry Prize, and represents the short list of the competition. The fifty poems in this monograph were selected by the editors, whose biographical notes can be found at the back of this book. Each was assigned the task of sorting through well over two hundred entries and selecting his or her favourite five. Author names were kept from the editors and no two editors looked at the same poems. With no haggling, no grading, no compromise, this collection is a book of favorites.

Happy reading!

Acknowledgements

Thanks to David Drummond for our marvellous cover design. And thank you to Simon Dardick and the Véhicule Press team for taking the trouble to produce and distribute such a handsome anthology. We'd like to acknowledge Peter Abramowicz's help and his continued support of this project. Thanks, too, to the members of the 2017 Editorial Board for their contribution to this global effort and for selecting the poems that appear in this anthology. Of course, none of this would be possible without the participation of those who entered the 2017 Montreal International Poetry Prize: we thank all of you for your interest and support. This year, the Montreal Prize lost one of its founding patrons, Leonard Cohen, who passed away in the autumn of 2016. This project would never have gotten off the ground without his generosity. Though we mourn his passing, we will continue to celebrate his magical *oeuvre* of songs and poetry.

Afternoons In and Out of Paradise

the loose-throated peals
of children playing, float across
fences, and into everyone's afternoon.

I remember one like this

shouts, climbing walls
crawling through keyholes
leaping into sick rooms

where he lay, dragging
his boated chest
over the barnacled air

spat into jars
raged as best he could
his wintering world

his wife calling out

turn down the volume
of our play, our high time
to scream

the afternoon scuttling itself

images of white sheets
disgusting jars
life at the other end, looming

incomprehensible

yet enough to haunt the ignorance
of our greenest days
uncomfortable with our plucked

fruit, yet comfortable with the distance

such a distance, a forever—
breathe in and out
and it's gone—

that afternoon like this afternoon

with the high spirits of children
thrilling the autumn
trees

I think of him, long gone

and ungrasped
by the scattering pirates, boarding
their backyard ships.

JULIE WATTS

The Art Gallery

Something brighter lives here
than the granite light
sparrowing in the arches—
a cathedralled order like a mind's
envisioning of itself.

The air in the vaulted cobalt walls
hangs sterilely, as if
a gurney were always just
disappearing around the corners
of the sloped causeways

aqueduct to dust to blue to how
solid the silence of winter
sky lathes down the halls'
white mortar of stone.
For every open door

another forty are closed,
sealed panels starch
as archivist's gloves
where you're certain
The Bureau Against Imagination

is busy with tin tools scratching
illuminations of night
into vials to be locked away
in drawers. Imagination grows
oranges bright as these lights

entreating us to grow
or else fall into a place like this
cloister at the gallery's end
where a gnarled tree wardens
a single gaunt plum.

It looks like the bronze spider
on the terrace crawled
sunk its fangs in the walls
torn as we are between
a painting of a sun in waves

and a drill-faced torso drilling
frantically at the blue dusted
dark until the moon slows
and the trees walk their seeds
through the broken windows.

CHAD CAMPBELL

An Attitude of Waiters

Eyes down, they won't see you.
Though it's only moments since
they pounced, so that you're seated
now. And now it is the season.
Let's have them stiff starched,
creased to bow, tuned to any tongue.
Their world is pigeon swift, yet
priestly, they will stand like herons,
have had the special training.
Collectively they know each
other's signs. Once of the kingdom,
it is we seek their attention. This is
as arduous as prayer. Patience! Are
we virtuous? Sometimes we wave
the scripture at them. Kitchen will
have none of that. Even the specials
run out. Clock slogs. Appetite
makes monsters. It will pauperize
the soul. Cook knows how much
condiment. To pay's something like
Ragnarök. It matters little how
much silver you leave for them
on the plate. In heaven one imagines
them, crowded to whim, obsequious
of any peep. No greater delight in
their station but serve. Of course
you are already fed. Nor will the savour
ever lessen. Here on earth, we're all as
much for form. My model's Charlie
Chaplin, with his two great buffet trays
and absolutely no intention to pay.
Cigar for after, that's the style.
And let the world cough up.

CHRISTOPHER (KIT) KELEN

Aubade

Karl foregoes jogging today, burps
the coffee carafe for one more slug
of umber pluck, and brief-cases, lunch-bags
it out the door, into the Sacramento sun,
the understoried sycamore and elm,
the hydrangea-blue skies. He pauses in the Subaru.
Wishes catch up with him, wannabes.
He's ariaed a few, poemed some.
Two cardinals red-shoe the bare oak limb,
red song, red wing. A phoebe tuxedoes the eave.
What they be, they do. Karl hums
the tenor part from Aida,
seconds the first tenor, keys
the ignition, sings and is singing.

MARY B. MOORE

Blanksicle

I count how many bedrooms ago
we ate fudgsicles after sex
on your balcony in Brooklyn. Four. Ferns
like the black fossilized wings
of dinosaurs. Your dad across the Hudson
inventing better and better
lightbulbs to flood ski hills at night. Fudgsicles
dripping into the street. Futuresicles. Pastsicles.
Nothing like presentsicles. Your fluorescent bra.
Your skin the colour of lemons
floating in a hotel pool at night. A truck full
of blood-vials crossing a bridge
to get analyzed. That's what I told your dad.
I didn't cross a bridge to get analyzed,
sir. Outside, a bird was making the sound
of a fax machine printing bad test results. I told
your mom she should get raptor
silhouettes to stop the bad news from slamming
into her windows. It started to rain
while you were in the shower. Tennis matches
were getting cancelled all over
the observable universe. I stood in the window
trying on the shape of an umbrella,
a popsicle stick, a fern.

DOMINIQUE BERNIER-CORMIER

Blue Curtains

The laundry curtains were pinned
together where the neckline
on a woman's blouse might be,

so that when my grandmother
stood behind them, her head
like hurried portraiture above

the pleated folds, or before them,
poised with a spilling armload
of clothes, I could never be sure

if she were, as it were, on the other
side, or had passed on through,
her blue shirt joined with a large

silver pin, but I was young, small
for my age and, if what my mother
says about my recollections

from the time are true, often
impressionable, and could reinvent
or painstakingly reinstall a scene

from the ground up, brokering
details I had witnessed with things
I'd imagined, which, as I was soon

to learn, is all you need to know
about the art of transformation,
so dialling in the season and year,

I can see my grandmother
behind blue curtains, or about
to part them, and in one variation

she turns, pegs in her mouth,
then runs back into the house
to where my grandfather, while

climbing back into bed, had
called her name out of surprise
or fright, as he had fallen.

ANTHONY LAWRENCE

Boa Gravida

When we were new,
our love still minnow-soft
and silver, you set their names
like nets along the water's edge.

Now the first, a son
surfaces, a great fish writhing
in the basket of my hips.

These last gravid days of rain
we digest the remains of years.

You speak of everything to come,
how you long to cradle the lotus-bud
of his skull in the broad leaf of your hand,
to swim in with him from the other side.

Until then, let us wait here in the restless earth,
whisper to each other in mangrove tongues.

Tell me I am beautiful and cold.
I will tell you how thirsty I am
for a mouthful of light.

At night I ache. Veins purple and rise
with this sudden season of blood.
Pelvic plates shift, bones shudder.

I am the great mother boa
turning the soft egg of the world
beneath my ribs. I will tear myself in two
and heal before morning.

DANIELLE BOODOO-FORTUNÉ

Caesura

I remember hearing about them, the babies   my Grandma never had,
and though I'd never held such a seed   in my body, I felt the want
of them. Five children with ghost-spaces   between. She believed
unbaptized souls went to Limbo,   which to me meant low,
so I saw them spread like mica   in the soil beneath her roses,
and in the gauze of grasshoppers   that rose with every step
through summer grass.   On my Grandma's ranch, I watched
a barn cat lick her living kittens   clean, leaving some still
sacked. Little grapes, their mother's   warmth unreplaced by their own.
When I bled, I locked the bathroom door.   Later, I pressed a still-
frame of my only ultrasound inside   my Grandma's copy
of *The Secret Garden*. Little unblossom,   little mausoleum.
I'm not religious anymore, but I grew up   with God,
the grandfatherly one who knew I was bad   sometimes,
but loved me anyway, and I could always talk to.   It's a hard habit
to break in the cathedral of my sleeping daughters,   that consecrated dark
gauzed in white-noise, a halo of nightlight.   My prayers are always
some variation of *Don't you dare*, and *Please*.   Somehow, I know he was a boy.
The middle brother. So little now,   so nothing. My daughters don't know
the word God. They know earth and death   and rain. They've watched
that silent sleight of hand replace   a caterpillar with an iridescent bud
of wings. They've seen me clutch   a spider between paper and a plastic cup,
only to crush a mosquito against   their bedroom wall, its body smeared
with our family's mingled blood.   They are learning to be merciful
doesn't mean to be good, only powerful   enough to choose.
After our cat died my oldest kept asking   *Where is she? I know she's dead*
but where is she? First, I spun a heaven-place,   then I changed my mind,
stood her barefoot in the garden and said   *Here, look down.*
The dirt is full of root and bone.   Oh, my darlings we are so small.
Lie down, back to summer grass. Feel   how we are always falling
into that star-spread black expanse.   And feel too
the way the earth holds us   and we are held.

Erin Rodoni

The Carnivores

say grace and photograph
the animals on their plates:
pink lamb and rare beef,
radioactive Fukushima fish,
so underdone they might get
up and walk or swim away.

Thanks and Amen.

While we name our martyrs, War
Children stopped in their tracks,

their flight patterns
are outlined in chalk
on streets where blood
flowers push through
pavement cracks, bomb
craters, sinkholes and
holes in the ocean,

their souls transposed
to yearning hybrids, algae
blooming and poppies
growing in killing fields
from Flanders to Damascus
to Sierra Leone, flesh so
underdone we might be
forgiven for thinking
prayer or shock therapy

might get them moving again.

Linda Rogers

Civil War at Parliament Hill Playground

"Come down: you aren't yet five!" She doesn't stir,
astride her look-out tower still, this spy
from the maternal camp; a rampart
of hands, of hair, defends her ears.

And all those other Sunday fathers, *mes
semblables, mes frères,* half-axed already, slumped
beneath a slide, must mount their one-way stair,
a scaffold's: here our executioners,
our daughters, aren't yet up for sliding down,
unless trumpets of pardon silver the sulky air.

JAMES GREENE

Degrees

Grandfather had a degree in English
Which he used to teach
Sonnets and soliloquies
To unsuspecting young men
And women who wanted
Degrees in English;
He died of a broken heart
When Grandmother whom
He kept under lock and key
To his bosom and other things,
Died. Mother keeps his degree
And a picture of him posing with it
Along with his death certificate
In a locker with her trinkets.
She has a degree in Math.

MAITHREYI KARNOOR

Esos Huesos (Them Bones)

> Horatio "El Negro" Hernandez, growing up in Havana,
> would cadge old x-rays from hospitals and use them to
> replace broken drum heads.
>   —*The Boston Globe*

He would play differently beating on a hip than he would
on a knee, the former deep and visceral, the latter light

and flexible. Ribs would bring to mind his grandfather
who'd broken six in a bar room brawl at seventy. When

rib x-rays began to crack beneath his pounding, he'd feel
the old man's pain. His sticks would run up and down

the length of foot bones—on those nights his playing would
devolve into a marathon where all he could do was put

one stick in front of the other until the club closed down.
Shoulder blades would make his drum sound like castanets,

fingers like the clatter of bamboo chimes. Skulls brought out
the best in him, made him play with intelligence and style

that complemented the balls of fire that were his hands.
On other nights he responded to the names on the x-rays.

Silvana Fernandez's long, slim femur infused his playing
with passion. Romario Diaz's dislocated shoulder

made his gestures loose and rubbery. The shattered skull
of Ernesto Lopez led him on wild, uncontrollable solos.

Later, when he was famous and could afford real drumheads
he missed the hundreds of companions who had accompanied

him to dim, dirty clubs, lent their bones to his music, felt
the rhythms of his heart's soft tissue down to the marrow.

LAWRENCE KESSENICH

A Father Shouldn't Cry

He shouldn't take your hand
on the red couch
the night before you have to leave
and as he talks
his large hand shouldn't
grasp your small hand
with the bitten nails
tighter and tighter
until it hurts

and you turn to look at him
his face clenched
his eyes filled with tears

even though grown-up men
don't cry
and you've never seen
a daddy cry before

because you have to leave him
to go three thousand miles
away, to a cold land
and now you've made him cry
and this is wrong

because everything is
upside down

and your father
who should be telling you
that everything will be all right

is telling you with his tears
that nothing will be all right
ever again.

Marsha Barber

Goya's Missing Skull

We never found it.
We never found them.

A polished mantelpiece, void of phrenology, absent its memento mori,
the rainbow-colored orbs in the pit at McDonald's PlayPlace

before Trayvon, before Tyre with his BB gun, before Gettysburg's opening volley
of cannon balls—bowling balls, Lebowski, Nam, M16s, magazines, Columbine,

a mallet-struck goat's head flicked across nomadic pastures,
stones and soccer balls skittering, blood-rust soil at Ghazi Stadium,

a sphere anchoring a sunken raft, an ovoid repast for fish
trawling the enticing edge of the undertow at Lesbos,

Mr. Kurtz's ivory globe—balanced in her ebony palm, the pilgrims squirting
pellets of lead, their Winchesters at their hips, he, almost dead,

Humpty Dumpty, the disembodied face of Oz, the Cheshire Cat
a floating   smile   reciting our most fearful nursery rhyme,

a crater in Homs, shaped like a cranium, where once lips kissed,
sipped laughter, cardamom coffee, orange-blossom water.

Nations decapitated, hurtling IEDs, the bunker buster Madar-e Bamb-Ha,
a blue marble spinning   desolate   in its intelligent universe,

the head still unaccounted for, the journalist from our close-knit hometown,
pinging date stones and olive pips, along with the others doomed,

a game of Risk to retrieve the world, a skein of dream-wool
saved for his sweater, wound tightly in a ball . . . disappeared

from Diane's worry basket of nights and days.
Poor Yorick's capital remains, sans soliloquy.

These were men, these were boys. These were women, these were girls
—their skirts twirled faster than dervishes, forming circles,

answering the grave-robbed past in the present tense, forever questioning.
We knew them. We trusted what went round-and-round inside their brains,

their senses sharpened, their voices battering Saturno,
his god-mad envy of his progeny. As gone as what cradled Goya's mind.

These are the time capsules we seek to find—swallowed into earth, sand, sea,
Munch's enigma, framing the letter O about to sound   in silent mimicry.

BARBARA HOBBIE

Guadalcanal

I

Neat as an Olympic diver, the moustached kingfisher
splits the brackish water, feathers luminescent tracer.

Akira watches the bird resurface, a fingerling in
its beak, long & silver as a newly crafted knife.

On an overhanging branch, it is devoured
in a few quick actions like cocking a rifle.

It scrapes both sides of its bill on a stem; mimics
a soldier cleaning his bayonet on some canvas.

His splash is small too. Like *Mbarikuku*, he is
holed up in the mountains, forced ever upwards

by the Marines who swarm over the island &
Henderson airfield like an invasive species.

II

The Corsairs make matchwood out of his gun pit.
He alone survives the bombardment. There is no

fire. The rainforest smothers any flame with its wet
blanket. Bones split; the trunks of downed canopy

giants that have collapsed under their dead weight.
Greasy sunlight patterns over him like camouflage.

Akira cannot hear the kingfisher's call. His
god rings a bronze Shinto bell in his head.

Purple berries rest by shell casings.
The bird's perch is a charred hand.

The enemy struggle to reach him.
Akira lets the leeches drink their fill.

III

At two thousand feet above sea level
the zoologist stumbles over a mystery.

He estimates the hole is coffin deep,
& precisely tooled by human hands.

He digs up the tiny lamps of shells &
rubs them. The trench is a good bird

hide to look for this rare species. On
a stump overhanging a creek he spies

a single male preening his molten head.
Azure wings like a Pacific island advert.

The kingfisher has telescopic sight, but
the mist net surrounds it like gun smoke.

He thinks of DDT & thin eggshells as
it cries; *ko-ko-ko-kokokokokokoko-kiew.*

B. R. DIONYSIUS

Here in White Swan

For Peter Ludwin

Tecumseh, Simcoe, Mission Roads.
Sad thing is I'm in my element.
A headcount would tally
more strays than locals
if you'd bother to keep track.
Pinkeye. Cleft palates. Head lice.
Now's the dog whipping hour,
for not coming when called,
for barking or not barking.
Nothing's better than nothing.
No taverns, no stoplights for 20 miles.
Our laundromat sells Pepsi, gas and Bud.
Malt liquor speeds up the intersection
of distemper with disbelief.
There's a log cabin church on the way
to Hoptowit's logging camp.
Its pews full only once
when the town was on fire.
Smoke shacks. Hop kilns. Wheel lines.
No cash or missiles in these silos.
No babes in our corncribs.
If you stay, you will taste silage
and failure. *Per capita* checks
land in the tribe's new casino.
Everybody's cousins. Sort of.
No natives dancing in the grange hall.
No Whites in Shaker Church.
Home of the PowWow Rodeo.
Home of the Grange Xmas Bazaar.
Home of—well—home.

Mint oil. Flat beds. Cattle guards.
Grazing rights all depend
on brace posts and barbed wire.
Bumper crops of buffalo grass
and sagebrush foretell
foreclosure. Stubble fields.
Alkali flats. DDT.
When our lumberyard gave in,
the white swans left the millpond,
never to return.

ALLEN BRADEN

Homestead

> Let the fox go back to its sandy den
> Let the wind die down. Let the shed go black inside.
> Let evening come.
> —Jane Kenyon, *Let Evening Come*

Alders, subtle but insistent, crowd the lane
Barbed wire guards raspberry and wild rose
Waist-high grass hinders humans
    and hides the fox
    creeping like a landlord
    among his butchery of bones
        Let the fox go back to its sandy den.

Big snows, rain and scorching summers
have worn away traces of the man who
    played the organ, cut wood
    a woman who baked bread
Wind blusters in the trees
    shushing echoes of children's voices
        Let the wind die down.

Only a shed remains that once held stern talks
    embraced calendars of bogus blondes
    displayed expired license plates
    a clutter of broken furniture
    nails, rake and a hoe
    now empty
        Let the shed go black inside.

Darkness may be a comfort
    please
        Let evening come.

ELIZABET STEVENS

How a Typo Changed the World

There has been a revolution in Darwinian Evolution:
Leading scientists have found buried deep, down underground,
A most shocking manuscript, locked away inside a crypt;
It's the last thing Darwin wrote; listen carefully as I quote:

"My great theory of evolution
Has suffered from a substitution:
Where *I* wrote "A"; *they* wrote an "I"—
Why, oh why, oh why, oh why!
Can't they get their spelling right!

People now run day and night,
Go on diets to lose weight—
Because of this malign mistake.
Survival of the *fittest* is not what I said!
If you're sinewy and skinny
You've been hideously misled.

Hear ye! Hear ye! One and all:
It's the fat, who have it all!
1869's the year I announced for all to hear
My great theory for survival
Of the fattest, the most idle.
A stupid "*I*" instead of "*A*"
Has sadly led the world astray.

Here's the science, here's the truth:
In order to survive your youth,
Bestow your genes on hale offspring
You must eat and eat; eat everything!
Survival of the fattest is the song to sing."

So, go and eat a fattening steak,
Followed by a cream-filled cake,
Then lie down all afternoon,
Lardy layers will pile on soon.

Throw away your diet book,
Stop exercising, always cook
With cream and butter afloat in batter,
In order to be healthy, you must strive to be fatter!

"Survival of the fattest," is our cry!
The fit, despite their strivings,
Will fail to fructify.

ANN GAMSA

I Am Not Born...

I am not born of Africa,
yet do I bleed for the horned
and tusked creatures of my never
homeland... raped and pillaged
for the myth of old men's virility.

I am not born of the polared vasts
that coat our northern lands,
yet do I hunger with the denizens
of that deep wasteland, watching, waiting,
as the ice recedes and their lives fade.

I am not born of the treed heights
that cradle the old men of the forests,
faces rimmed with flame as their homelands burn,
bodies of their mothers and young etched
in the fire of man's greed.

I am not born of the ocean's depths,
sonared cries echoing grief beyond gauge
with each butchered breath, heart strings tortured
past telling to deafened ears... tears upon tears
disappearing in salted waters.

I am not born of this world of gouging gain
that pits peopled plains against every grace that gifts
this precious planet... I am not born of this, cannot bear
the burden of pain or pacific plenty... my soul
rebels... rebukes... reborn, reaches... for more.

I am not born of Gaia's get. My stuff is not the stuff
of this earth, but finds its home, its heart, its heritage
in the sweet beyond, One with the Morning Stars,
singing its soul's song with the Sons and Daughters of God,
in mourning for this sad, sweet Earth.

And yet... and yet... here am I.
Striving, still, to heal this hurt and harried heart,
here among the fallen... angels all... my brothers,
my sisters, my sentient soul, suffering...
still harried, still harnessed, still... here.

JNANAMA ISHAYA

Kaieteur Falls (Potaro River, Guyana)

> Out of curiosity, our physician on location...wanted to see the mysterious nesting place of the swifts.
> From the bottom of the falls, the gigantic cave is inaccessible...We lowered a camera to him...
> Later, we decided not to show his footage [due to the wishes of the local people].
> —*The White Diamond* (2004), Werner Herzog

In that scene, there were swifts that live in a cave
behind a waterfall. At daybreak, they would fly

out through the water, murmur into the shape
of a monstrous grackle, feathers flickering black

iridescence. The dark shape spins and explodes
to a blurred pixilation in our mind's frame.

Again and again they coalesce and split into waves,
unroll as giant arabesques that curve against

the screen of the sky. We are made to hover
over the paper white of the mist. It shimmers

in the sunlight, forms a rainbow at its belly.
The water pours from a point so high, we never

question its power, never look up, and we cannot
see what ends below. In the distance, mountains

fluoresce, clouds pump their heartbeat colours
while through all this, the water continues

its endless spitting. There is nothing else to bear
while that moisture clings to our skin. Sometimes

we can glimpse the cave when the wind gusts
and billows the fall. The sheet lifts, folds, shows us

the open mouth. The sky begins to darken, and they return.
Now their sound becomes a mass that wraps into a point:

watch how they unravel to form a snake of coal dust
that plunges through the fine spray, into the hollows,

until the tail whips across to snap the curtain shut, smooths
white noise of water over the silence of sleeping birds.

Fawzia Muradali Kane

My Ill-Omened, Mid-Life, First and Last, Southern Wedding

I had a hunch it might happen while collecting our licence.
Why else wear his boxer shorts beneath my blue dress
and new coat, Nana's ring on a finger that didn't count?

Glass window paperwork at City Hall—our mothers' first
and middle names the same. *Unusual*, said the clerk.
The judge is in. Would y'all like to do it now?

I ran outside in deep winter to pluck any bouquet,
returned with a sprig of holly berries, pricking,
praying myself blind to symbolism.

From a waiting room like some old dentist's,
a policeman delivered us to the judge. I hung
back. The officer la-la'd *Here Comes the Bride*.

It went like in the movies, but I stumbled at the part
about parting: *To* death do us part, more like a toast.
Wanting to believe not the same as believing.

Signed, stamped, embossed, entered. His mother's ring
loose on my finger. *Are you saying my mom has big hands?*
Into the car to a pizza bar for a guestless, giftless dinner.

Arriving, my left hand on the door—bare! Panicked
scrabble through foot-well trash, the sunset rush
back to City Hall's gutters, luckless muddy grass.

All that looking down instead of up. We tried a
better restaurant. A Georgia Peach, then I was served
the wrong meal; the right one late, lukewarm, lacklustre.

Across town to his buddy to beg weed and moonshine.
The wife, post-surgery wan, took our wedding photo
in the basement den, silhouettes against dim light.

Left to right: her unfaithful husband; mine grinning harder
than before or after; me, ringless; and, soon-to-be-dead,
the lodger—best man there, turns out—holding a shotgun.

Found the ring in the car next day, wore it on my thumb.
Left it behind in the bathroom when I flew home to Mum.
He lost his job and hocked it before a year was done.

Lauren Williams

Ode to My Period

> In Cantonese, women tell each other,
> *Yi ma lai doh*: My great aunt has come to visit.

My "great aunt" rarely visits

now but she found me in Sichuan

half way up the slope of Er Mei Shan.*

I was on the way to the peak

with four other women when great aunt beckoned

the monkey to leap from his leaf nest

in the mountain camphor tree onto

my pack full of apples. The monkey bared his fangs

when we shouted and waved our arms.

He lifted the pack flap and reached in for two pieces of

fruit. Then later, the raven that sauntered into

the women's toilet in the monastery garden

didn't fly away when I squatted over the stone hole,

plucked my used pad from the bin. He ambled

outside, scattered scarlet petals

of its blown blossom on the breeze.

Great aunt has retired since that climb,

but sends notes in the beak of

a dark bird. The stain of her sunset returns

after an afternoon of love.

> * Buddhist holy mountain in Sichuan province.

KATE ROGERS

Odile, The Black Swan

Impossible to look at her without thinking dark water, depths
where light doesn't reach. In the diner on Dalhousie,
her presence commands the booth, though only the decrepit

at the counter sees the water rising, water-
line gurgling just beneath her chin. Flutter
of a dark wing that briefly stretches. Sally, a regular, orders

coffee between johns, eggs at 4 a.m. They arrive, sunny side
silicon perfect. Minivans line up to glean sorrow
from her eyes. If only I could dance, says Sally. When the sky

turns pink, she'll sleep. Odile once had an act involving lit black
candles and a snake. Smoke she could conjure on demand.
Rose on stage, an angel from the black lake.

They all desired her, but one. Before Champagne Rooms,
loose laws, when looking was enough—
She holds her mug as if it could contain her.

The transistor radio tin-tin-tins demented heart songs
tie a yellow ribbon… and getting caught
in the rain… and I'll never have that recipe again…

Pale-skinned fries rise like broken limbs from plates, tendrils of vinegar
seep down. The scent is grease, acid, hot breath and chrome.
There are no new ways to be alone. There are no new ways to mourn.

Una McDonnell

Old Blue Suitcase

Every morning when I'd take that walk
I'd see her with her old blue suitcase.
I didn't know where she'd been that night,
but the suitcase always managed to get her back.
At the foot of the stairs to the side of the coffee shop.
Someone always bought her a cup,
their good deed taken care of before 7 am.
Then the suitcase could start its day.
The corner torn open, one wheel missing,
but still functional as a suitcase and
a chair, a table, a bed, a weapon.
When the sun reflected off something on a high ledge
her curiosity got the better of her and that suitcase became a ladder.
The stray piece of metal was worthy,
carefully placed inside the front pocket of old Blue.
Once when I was waiting for the bus,
that suitcase appeared at my side. I'd never seen it that close.
That was the first time I heard her voice,
she asked if I could spare a smoke.
We shared the quiet ritual like old friends,
but we always seemed to exhale at different times.
She asked me my name then wandered off before I could answer.
I tucked the pack of smokes under the handle,
I was sure she wouldn't mind.
One day I found the suitcase sitting alone.
At the foot of the stairs to the side of the coffee shop.
I left it for three days, just to be sure.

CHLOE SPARKS

On the Other Side Of An Hour

Let's say you had known then what you know now:
on that morning you came to visit your friend at home,
even when you knocked on his door, let's say you'd known
when you entered his room that he would already be gone:
let's say you held a mess of wildflowers in your arms;

you had brought the blooms to improve the atmosphere,
to lay them along his quiet body and in so doing draw
communion to him and the slow opening of stained petals
spread along his forearm and stretching to his bare shoulder
where you imagined he would have placed them himself.

Let's say instead of losing, or held at bay as you were,
you had traced the loose map he kept guarded in his mind,
a private reckoning that laced, like stars, *a* to *b* to *c*—let's say
you had seen it all so clearly it was as if you understood:
the end, the beginning, love, the cockeyed cedar tree.

AMBER MCMILLAN

Overture

By cock and bull, tooth and oxidized nail
you will whistle like Harpo Marx
while I write *La Symphonie de C'est Fini*.
The notes ricochet off the crags of your heart
as magnetic North guides tall ships to breach the waves,
before the topple of sails, being swallowed by endless sea.
A certain lifeline for one, it was tidily hidden
in your back pocket when we were dry-docked.
I thrash and recall old dreams of porpoises,
know why I learnt to swim at four in the cold of Blackstone Lake,
one finger touching bottom before racing towards light.

You pointed it out with a laugh, liking the linguistics,
how "lover" without the "L" becomes "over"
until it rose like an overture, a watery muffle of music
to break hardened earth, as if for gentle burial.
I replied with "Over/kill."

Overtures are the sly, impish passes you made
when your kitchen-handy wife reached low for the meat platter,
put x-ray vision on old Harris lines in her bones hidden by a long skirt
your sour/sweet mouth twitching over a Gilbey's gin bottle
in a live commercial your friends watched without buying,
me, having the coin to try the package and susceptible
to the subliminal encased in extraterrestrial signs,
a figurine in a snow globe floating unanchored in a styrofoam sea.

By the buffet table you motioned to me like Marcel Marceau
with your palms miming the movement up a staircase
to show me your love in a familiar but locked place
and I glimpsed funhouse distortions in the vanity mirror
before you came down to whistle like Harpo.

Through cracks there plays a scrimmage between ritual,
the scissoring open of shrink-wrapped goods from Ikea and
being stuck like a bad investor in a bear market,
until the slight push of one domino against another, as it will at 29 tiles,
gains enough momentum to make the Empire State Building fall.

This is physics. It is all seasons. It is the invitation of spring
flourishing with dewy buds, showcasing into summery green,
eviscerating the leaves by autumn with the last blazing color.
When winter comes, by the barren of its snowy landscape there is no shock,
the symphony of our own construct now lapping us to sleep.

Karey Willan

Return of the Spider Mother

After Louise Bourgeois

You don't have to be cloistered
in a darkened room, crouched over a candle,
to summon her. You don't have
to make a scene, smash crockery or draw
any attention to yourself.

Only allow your anxiety to grow,
spiralling out of you in lines
that cover the walls of white corridors,
and outside are skeins of a broken web
caught on a barbed wire fence.

She knows that you need her,
picked up on your distress signal,
her eyes snapping open,
head swivelling on its smooth gears.
You've waited long enough.

Listen out for her spiked heels
clacking over the flagstones towards you.
Be ready to hold out your arms. Together
you'll rise as high as a steeple, steadied
on pincers locked into the pavement cracks.

She will come back. She's on her way,
the good mother, the fierce mother.
With her needle and thread, she'll repair
all that came undone,
the sky, your lacerated heart.

DAVID MARK WILLIAMS

San Vigilio de Marebe

In the piazza of San Vigilio we sit talking, two old men,
about nothing, about the beauty of nothingness and
the way things were before the coming of the tourists,
who come in the time of lemons, who come in the time

of grapes ripening, who come with their Rolex watches
and their Gucci luggage taking photographs of two old
men talking on a quiet afternoon with the sun on them,
the mountains behind them, about the olive trees and

how they came early this year not late like last year,
how perfectly round and sweet they are like oranges
in Gubbio at the end of summer when all things turn
older but still sweet as a kiss of the sun on your hand

when you're sitting and talking, just two old men about
nothing, about the beauty of nothingness, how lovely
the mountains are in Marebe when the sun is behind
them, still they come with their Rolex watches and their

Gucci luggage taking photographs of two old men of no
importance who go out to the orchard in the afternoon
when light between the boughs of the olive trees casts
long shadows, what are they searching for, what do they

think we know, a secret, two old men talking about nothing
the sun on our backs the mountains behind us, yet there is
a lingering light in the afternoon we sometimes pause for
and remain mute in the presence of, a form of worship

some could say, a secret kept between us unspoken but
understood, the divine nature of afternoon light that hovers
over the olives so sweet and perfectly round like the bosom
of women when they get out of bed or bathe their hair in

secret, there are things we know without knowing them
that are secret but we don't speak of them, only of the
olives coming early this year and the beauty of nothingness
that even the agony on the face of St. Vigil in the Duomo of

Marebe cannot capture exactly.

RICHARD JAMES

Seasonal Affective Disorder

I answer winter with Florida,
Blue Moon beermosas, swamp
pontoon rides, fishy pelican breath.
As good a place as any
to drink myself to death.

Clouds piss themselves, rain
slamming mint and lilac
motels, palms, plastic
surgery billboards asking,
Are your cups half empty?

Fearing falling coconuts, I pull over
and watch two gators make tender,
minimalistic love in a ditch. I imagine
my skin thickening to gator hide.
As good a gamble as any
to hide from the future,
to make my life continuous

prologue. Hibiscus open their dumb
fuchsia throats to the humidity.
Hungover, I eat cold noodles
out of a styrofoam clam.
I stroll on damp, gritty sand,
picturing the melancholy
and mystical sex lives inside
those rainbow sherbet houses
precarious on stilts.

Veering between the drunks
blasting beer and truck country
and the drunker drunks blasting
breakup country, I step on something
sharp. A clamshell, or part of one.
Ridged blush, cream, orange, tinged
with blood, as good a sunset.

CATRIONA WRIGHT

Sewing

Each darting plunge
like fortune's wheel—
the bobbin spinning
to her toe's touch,

her tongue locked
between front teeth—
such concentration
held our lives in check;

or when she'd baste
my sister's puff sleeve
or hung nautical drapes
to keep nightmares out,

she'd snip a length
as if to cut a cord,
then pull a seam
to test its strength

on a wear-worn dart.
Piece by patient piece,
she fashioned our lives,
a Singer, her delicate art,

racing to beat the light,
dancing on heads of pins,
repeating patterns of memory,
until line held tight.

BRUCE MEYER

Snow Crabs

The crabs *are* there, melting into
their familiar habitat, fallen on
zoology's harder times, patient
yet pure as the driven snow.
They are seldom seen by anyone
because no one ever speaks of them.
They are fauna's seedless Clementines
before the word for orange was said.
Like memory of what has no name,
they bear the invisible weight of time.
They eat the silence of a hidden life.
Like a zodiac sign after daybreak,
or the silent truth below ocean storms,
they love in white and delicate bodies
masked from everything but a name
and multiply throughout the winter,
learning to sting in a veil of ice.
They count among the raw spring stars.
They pince the sun until it melts them.
A lone streetlamp cranes its neck
to count the diamonds of their eyes.

BRUCE MEYER

Soldiers

Sunsets, Dad and I walked the dog around the block
and he told me all about his journeys, the places
he'd been in his life. The 'twenties and 'thirties were great
until the Depression even then you got by, tough times all right.
Then there was the war when the world turned to shit.
Your war memories amazed me most, kitted out in jungle green
how tough you had to be, diving off a sinking troopship
when it hit a mine, sleeping with your rifle
strapped to a tall tree above the Borneo forest canopy.
The glory of war: weeks behind enemy lines without shower
or latrine, the food tasted like murder and the morphine
wasn't strong enough when they got the shrapnel
out of your back. There was that one time you were shaving
that one time you were shaving outside the tent, about 5 am
before the day's heat and mugginess settled.
Reflected in the tin shaving mirror you see a glint of metal
in the bush that shouldn't be there, the flash from a sword,
katana, or whatever they call it (you almost laughed the words)
you kept shaving and watched in the mirror
the Japanese soldier moving quickly, quietly towards you
all you're armed with is a cut throat razor—it'll have to do—
he creeps up and as he draws the sword from its hilt you spun around.
Stunned and terrified the bastard cried *mama*—one fluid
movement like a flattened forehand tore the soldier's larynx out
as he fell he looked into your eyes, he was just a boy
maybe seventeen or eighteen, did not have a blessed hope.
Afterwards you carried the sword in your kitbag.
The jungle heat was powerful, kind of life-affirming
in spite of the killing, and the malaria would stay in you
and keep these days to relive in future fever dreams, and sweat
turned your bed into a swamp. You shouted and swore in English
and Japanese the fury of killing and living

it was like being back there with you in that godawful war
as we cooled our dad's burning head with damp towels.
Waking you'd stare and cry for the poor Japanese soldier
and his mama. The sword lay on the wardrobe floor,
next to a laundry basket.

S. K. KELEN

Song from Cadiz

What do I care
if one team wins?

If the night is warm and wet,

Let's hunt snails!
Let's live together!

tri li li, onward...

Come to my table, salt shaker,
don't hide, I've already seen you
a long ways back
I've got crystals and herbs
aye, lad
I have wax and it's from bees
marbles blown of glass
sheep skins and salt—
plenty of salt,

but these lines to Mirabrás

are for you and you only
I started them
when
      I saw you from afar

Zoe VanGunten

Song of the Water Lilies

Have you ever watched a Water Lily grow?
They are creatures of the light.

Slowly, they unfold their bodies and   offer
their scented song   to the world.

Light does that—gently pulls   the music
out of you, rendering you (weightless)   yet
full as a hive of raw, unadulterated   honey.

I am standing at a cliff's edge—
arms open wide like a man on a cross—ready
to be delivered   from the weight of things.

Time has worn me like a favorite pair of jeans
and now there are more   holes   in me   than songs,
more air   in me   than warmth.

I am cold   always cold. My flesh   has reached
its limit and now cries in the night for the clock   to stop
his wielding   of cruel hands.

Have you ever heard such a sad song? I look at the birds
and envy the confidence they hold in their own wings,
the joy they express in the finding   of a grovelling worm.

But the pieces of my heart are steadfast still—   they wait
for the wooing   of the light.   Soon, it will rise and pour
like a jar of honey over me and I will be covered—
resurrected—
in sweet   sticky   delight.

My holes will become holy and my cries
will blossom into songs   of victory.

Have you ever tasted such a song?
Richer than King Solomon, fuller than the fiery bush
or the ancient land as it wept waters of destruction,
where only   faithfulness   could save you?

I am young   I am weak   but I am learning:
    the song of the Water Lily only rises
after receiving   the light.

Abigail Wieser

The Story of Us

As is the custom with starting new things, I am doing this not well but with the intention of improving. This you & me, which we may as well call **us**—this face to face & heart & lung(s) & other vital organs we'll be needing for this trip, most impressively in your case brain (& please do notice how I flatter you here because it may be some time before I do that again)—as terrifying as that sounds, & is, & will be, feels to me to be nudging like a fat tender grub towards something not uncomfortable, towards not gross, inching its way into the fragile world of light & air & utter transience. It is a feeling not standard.

I am a pretentious little thing, including & especially in relation to matters of the aforementioned vital organs—i.e. heart, lung(s), brain—& I feel the kidneys, too, deserve mention here, given their job of filtering out all the crap. I imagine there will be plenty of that ahead of **us** on account of **us** both being human 'n all, ergo, fully weird.

Or is it the liver? & what the hell is a pancreas? Perhaps if I had listened more instead of undressing with my eyes the man I will simply refer to as Mr Biology (albeit my execution was meticulous). Cellularly speaking, he remains not insignificant—which is more than can be said for the box of frogs he had us dissect & spear (in not that order). There's nothing quite like that timeless combination of amphibian death & bad aftershave to stir the primal lustings of a thirteen-year-old. I am sorry in advance for all the crap your organs will be required to deal with. & I will just add here in my defence that failing science is a long-standing family tradition (with the exception of Phil the doctor who we mostly don't talk about, hence the parenthesis).

Anyway, this is me saying hopelessly hopelessly but with what I hope you will assess to be a commendable level of enthusiasm that I am more than moderately impressed with the start we have made, despite my opening gambit & notwithstanding our various inadequacies, idiosyncrasies & other nouns which makes **us** sound more complete than we currently are. The thing is, I think that together, in time, we might become so—that in time you might teach me important things such as how to use words like 'antecedent' & 'diaspora' for reasons other than fashion or fear, & that I might teach you things, mostly smiling-related, such as how to smile at a leaf & at not winning the lottery & at good things happening to bad people such as bad people winning the lottery, & that together we will grow worthy. & armed with this shared knowledge, this shared worth, we will go forth & make a story which we will breathe into the eversphere so those passed into energy may admire **us** for our valour & our pluck, & blow: Well done.

Isn't it funny how verbs are called doing words & adjectives are called describing words etc. when presumably all words are just trying to be themselves? Perhaps we should just let them be—or at the very least stop typecasting them.

I also apologise for my insistence on believing that my casual (mis)use of language in some intangible but charmingly hipster way heightens my appeal. I hope to soon grow out of this. For now, I will sing along the exceedingly long floorboarded hallway of our soon-to-be house & at a certain point, just here, I will stop. to listen. to the story of **us**. Are there children? Are there cakes with candles? Is there loss? Are all the usual too strange too wonderful things of life present?

ANNA MURCHISON

Stranded Conch, Alabama Coast

Not quite beached but perched
on a sandbar yards from shore;
water only inches deep
bares the conch to air
and cormorant and gull.

Tipped by surf it lolls,
flesh-side up, shell in sand,
and writhes to right itself,
its meat the dense, freckled
pink of a piglet's tongue.

A blot resembling mussel-shell disrupts
the pink—*operculum,* I'll learn:
a door the conch shuts fast
when it retreats and seals itself
inside its fabled home.

We two in swimsuits huddle, gape
and prod—until a snort
from the shell's long siphon states
the creature's urgency to self-propel
to deeper water. So I push it free.

We stand. Backs ache
from stooping, shoulders from the sun.
Country music booms onshore:
a man acquired a woman, built a home—
or lost those things. I'm never sure.

We wade back to the land.
We carry buckets of the shells
we've picked up—polished, vacant, bright.
The living conch has veiled itself in sand
and sealed its doorway tight.

Peter Norman

Syzygy (Scrabble with Ivy)

Edge, swerve, disturb, you're all
verb: pressed to you, wilfully
irresistibly, like ivy, sighingly, I climb like
an adverb unattached, insouciant, this high
wire, thighs and strive, brine and hive, like
glide and tine: riskily, out along the wire
wildly shuffling the letters I have to find
my lines, a sign: my evergreen, my ground-
creeping, my *hedera rhombea*, my
araliaceae, my nouns, my verbs, my rising
to scale these outcrops, my um-
bel, my unlobed adult leaves, my
fertile flowering stems, my
marginal list of small words to hold

the edges of other words, fold
into yours like buds or lovers, and my
you are fine, high-scoring, blithe, you
spell out my secret names (bind-
wood, lovestone), syllables
no one uses except to access this
bingo, palmately, this lucky hand, this
random allocation, all squiffy squeeze, as I sigh
against artery and inferior rib in the crush
of these tiles and us, defying windfall damage, my
greens deepen, words like birds arrive
to disperse seeds like leaves, until my—
like a happy hand of letters, like
za or qi—and quixotry—this syzygy.

FELICITY PLUNKETT

The Wall Said

The wall said
"The Cloudy River Gang"
in red;
I'm certain of the color
but the words change when
I look back;
the first two words framed within
an otherwise unspoiled patch of wall,
a patch long preserved
by a newly absent fixture;
"River Gang" was passed over
by the shadow of a bobbing branch;

elsewhere in the same house,
I snap a picture of a shattered pink toilet,
then recline along the floor,
taking in the glue and nails, the joints
and tags that mark the underside
of furniture and cabinets and counters;
I disrupt and rearrange
the floor's unaccountable grit
with each pivot of perspective;

as I drove away
to the next scheduled location
the windshield was crossed
into a sequence of spaces
that offered the day's photos
for review; images accurate enough
to recall the negatives

slumbering in my camera
and transparent enough to reveal
the road rushing forward,
ecstatically aligned.

DEREK SUGAMOSTO

The Ways

When you wake, and again when you get home, walk out
into the cold and go round the farm.
Just walk. Think nothing, but know your breath
is bringing in the outside.

It begins as an adventure, to be alone.
The wind coming in from Antarctica
is company enough of an evening,
cutting cold across the paddocks.

But somehow, it stirs you up
as the old gumtrees flinch and creak,
their damp leaves winnowing free;
seized, just as you are, by something.

Go stand on the stone helmet of a hill
or in the plunging midst of a paddock of grass.
Stand in wait for an idea of yourself
that seems as if it might grow steadfast.

Keep turning to take in the horizon as it slips
away and think again about what lies
beyond vision, past the ways you know
of how trees bend and wind moves across the waves.

Do this as if in preparation, for you know not what
will come afterwards. Follow along the ways
where you've walked before,
going into what you have come out of, again.

MARJORIE MAIN

They are Drawn Here In the Springtime

For Mariel Hemingway

Perhaps they were orchids, as if Theodore Roethke
had been called here in the dead of night, drunk again

wandering into the yard through a broken fence, in darkness—
past the swing set, past the hammock, past the children's

stray toys, past the plastic trays of daisies, and the small
carefully folded envelopes of wildflower seeds:

to the garden, planting orchids under the apple trees;
those loose, ghostly mouths: I am dreaming; she laughs, smiles.

My wife is planting flowers. But late that night, in the quiet
cool hours near dawn, smooth, delirious roses sing the delicate

dream of her skin to my lazy fingers; my hand touches orchids
in moonlight just dreamt, falling, and falling, and falling

through her long, long hair. "Orchids—"
"Yes—"

BRUCE VAN NOY

The Thieves Have Gone

Left less than traces. Bestowed a quality of absence,
invisible like fingerprints. 'Justice is an art of theft,'
Plato's Homer says. It took us time to know they'd been.
So many toys in the cupboard! It's negative theology.

You sense something, go on until you know they've gone
through the whole house. One can only imagine the frenzy
of greed. Is there even adrenalin? Police say that they
took their time. You're still really not sure what's missing.

Have to make a claim. The company knows that you'll
go on discovering things not there for years. And
not discovering. Some things you'll never know were
gone. This means that you had already moved on.

It's like that with the model aeroplanes mother threw out
because they gathered dust, then grit. How long until grief
came to them—and how long did that last? For years
the echo goes on this way—a death far off in the family.

Makes you wonder how it is to be raped, think what torture
is to survive. How little our losses we first-world-most
to whom more always comes. This little theft that stays
with you makes precious what you have. It's all so long

ago now, what's gone so inessential. Still you see them
gloating on, enjoying always what was yours. Makes you
think what it is to lose a country, to be banished, to escape
just with your skin. Now elsewhere of yourself, you must

make another meaning. Will you find welcome? You
don't forget. Every theft is with us. We are the past piled
up. You wonder about the country located right now
underfoot. It's personal, the passage of time, like

the color of your language. You find yourself looking
sometimes suspiciously in the street. Is that someone
stranger playing old records? Does he/she wear my ring?
We know to be better than that however. First curse

forgiveness reconsiders. Can parties unknown be redeemed?
Anyway, the old theft's not so different from your own
packing up to go. What you've lost is just as you. It's only
the remembered missed. We're privileged with a choice in

such matters as—why come, why part, whether to return.
You see yourself sitting in the empty room, time vanished
here because you took it. Not far off the mystery's solved.
So all along and after all at least you were a thief too.

CHRISTOPHER (KIT) KELEN

The Time White Lightning Busted Out

Inside our guts a jitter.
Inside the jitter a ribbon
the color of a January morning
curling past the wood box
and through the shed door,
to the packed dirt floor,
the rusted-out hinge.
Inside a velvet black
the empty water bowl
and inside that lack
a lost pony in a blizzard,
out on the hill or down
a two track to the river
winding along our worry,
the frozen car battery,
'til finally our tires
slip the slant road
to the high pasture.
We scour the storm—
ice crystals hurtled
through the eye of a needle,
threading our hearts
with gleanings of tracks
beside the snow fence.
And inside those tracks
recognition, a small hope.

CYNTHIA HUGHES

Tranquil

I'll probably cut this line,
maybe this one, too, and the next,
the one that describes the blanket—
it's no good, you keep it,
the line, I mean, though you can have
the old blanket, too, whose rough wool
scratched us all winter on that couch
you've taken with the music and the Terrier,
leaving only a few unmatched dishes
and a memory I no longer want:
the day the snow surprised the city—
you at one end of the park,
me at the other, dog by your side,
the spot we were to meet in the middle
an objective correlative of all compromises
with which we would surely collude,
the whole silly city out shovelling,
the white world masquerading
as some sort of moment—take it all, crate it
up with the photos, pop it all in the boot
along with all that we once felt
for one another, take everything
but this poem you'll never see
me cut line by line:
fold, spindle, mutilate—it's going,
you're in charge, my queen, my subject
no longer, once I've cut these last few
about the books we'd planned to read, the dog
I'll tell you now I hated, the day I can't stop
thinking about, which ended with a blanket,
an old couch, and started with the snow
laid out between us like this cold, blank page.

BRYAN WALPERT

Twenty-two Days Before the
First One Hundred Days

The first camera I recall holding was the Polaroid Land Camera, that
    old grey mare, the Highlander,
with its rare roll film that developed in the back, but I wouldn't have
    known that then, what I knew,
when I was five, was how to fondle the black vinyl bellows that
    protected the light as it flew
from lens to caught frame, how to slide the Chrysler-chrome hood of
    the aperture along its metal track,
out to the world to see something, then back into the steel case, click,
where seeing clear would be closed down and kept so safe, the ivory
    dial with its red and certain arrow choosing
between two shutter speeds. Henry Dreyfuss. He designed it. 1954.
    One year on and
Dreyfuss, who would before he killed himself at love's height in a
    suicide with his dying wife give us
the Bell phone, the John Deere tractor, the Westclox alarm clock that
    sent us each into those needful morning shifts,
before he spent his whole life lifting a little elegance into our half-lived
    twentieth-century,
he wrote his opus, *Designing For the People,* the people!—the dream
    that part of any machine's purpose was to be
human experience. It's New Year's Eve, eve, again, I'm in a LaQuinta
    Inn in Macon, Georgia.
I don't know how to say out loud the count of Confederate flags I saw
    on the way here. Sold out,
they put me in a smoking room fashioned in cheap contemporary
    with two bowed beds and my dog keeps itching.
I'm driving back from Christmas with my mom, who moved to
    Florida once she got rid of us, who lived her happy life there,
who this week asked which of her rings I want when she dies. I don't
    want her to die. I don't want

Carrie Fisher to die or Debbie Reynolds to die a day after Carrie Fisher
    dies. I don't want my mom to know
who Debbie Reynolds is and me to know who Carrie Fisher is and for
    neither of us to know who the other
is talking about. I don't want 2017 or 2016. The ball has dropped a
    hundred times: Prince and Bowie,
Leonard Cohen, the Wizard of Woo, Gwen Ifill, Phife Dawg,
    Dr. Stanley, Christenberry, Eli Wiesel,
Tupac's mom, my boss's Grandado, Ali, democracy, for Christ's sake,
    Dreyfuss! Save us! The rapture is on
and all the elegant ones are leaving. Build something, a worthy thing
    for which they'll want to stay, build a way
for us to see clear through this our winter of disconnect, build a steel
    case to click. I want two speeds. Dials to turn.
I want the human experience of metaphor and not a metaphor of
    experience. I want the ruby and diamond gold estate ring
on my mom's hand, her hand in mine, the two of us walking into a
    store to look at bobbles, so pretty, that we will not buy.

REBECCA GAYLE HOWELL

Walk Along the Berlin Wall

In Berlin once there was a brick wall
carving the city in two, a knife
through the heart of a country, the heart
of its people, the heart of a world.
From 1961-1989, a thick wall of bricks
said more than any fevered king ever had, crying

*you can't go there, quit your snivelling crying
or else.* Barbed wire adorned the top of the wall
keeping everyone on their side of the bricks.
Over 5,000 attempted escape, nothing but a knife
and the sweaty clothes on their back. The world
consumed the over 100 who died. It is said a heart

can physically break from pain. How many hearts
were lost? How many died before death, left crying?
How many lovers who had made a world
of themselves were left with empty hands? The wall
was 77 miles of no, towers with guns and knives
at the ready. To many, the wall was not brick.

It was the layering of a philosophy, like stacked bricks,
It was the deliberate calcification of one's heart
for the "greater good," a new Germany, the gentle knifing
of a collective spirit, a will that brushed off crying
and laughter, those pesky mosquitoes, on one side of the wall.
The sun blazed and baked down upon two different worlds

for thirty years. In 1987, David Bowie showed the world
its own ugly self at a concert in West Berlin—the bricks
still intact. We can be heroes, he sings, to those over the wall
in East Berlin, to a pulsing, bleeding mob of hearts

who just want to be free, an end to the dulled crying
in their hollow bones. The music was a blistering, thick knife

to the gut. The German word for knife
is *das Messer*. Yes, we all made a mess of the world.
But, sometimes, the naked act of crying
can cleanse. Sometimes not. Some moments, like bricks,
stiffen in the brain. Some people never master their hearts.
Today, beautiful art covers one side of the fragmented wall.
In the end, knives couldn't keep love from destroying the wall.
A country cried and dripped happy tears onto smashed bricks.
A world bled together, pumping yes through its patched, moaning heart.

AIMEE MACKOVIC

When My Father Met Jesus

One evening the living room walls folded
>   down around him, and Walter Cronkite's voice
unspooled to a wave thinning into blackness.

A star grew from the sky and landed in the yard,
>   a figure emerged. He could tell by the hair
it was Jesus, a certain brightness to the eyes.

My father stepped over the sill of the house
>   and walked with Jesus into the fields
down where the stream crosses the road.

They talked about their battle scars:
>   the betrayal of their fathers,
a sponge of vinegar, malaria in the Philippines.

They discussed how to feed the hungry
>   and love your enemies.
Why worry about your life? Seek first the kingdom of God.

He returned to the couch then for another fifteen years,
>   ranting, *Love your neighbor, dammit!*
And *I come not to bring peace but a sword!*

In his last days in the hospice room at the V.A.
>   he asked me to scribe for him, his voice
barely a whisper, but he wanted to get this part down.

So I typed the words fast as I could,
>   letters lifting off the paper,
love reeling around our heads like little black stars.

CYNTHIA HUGHES

Wild Horses

Haphazard, hulking, & hideous,
    the weathering of switch-houses & well-houses
girdling the train-trestle's girders.
    What gray railroader welded hours
on end to anchor this ancient bridge?—
    an after-thought now to all but the walleye, hares,
martins, & those, like us, who must cross its truss
    hoping to manage a glimpse of wild horses.
Across the river, the rocks, even, are running to rust,
    ransacked by taggers, who wiled hours
marking up the monoliths with sappy glyphs. I hate them,
    mostly, though the impulse still pulses: to wield hearts
without restraint, without regard—desire rising, & risen,
    writ in a red so ardent the walled heats
of their scrawlings should've burst into flame
    or bloom or the braying of wild horses
at first sight. But they don't. Instead, they sit, squat
    on the shelf of sediment, below wheeled houses
of stars which turn, turn, turn, & so I saw
    love demands stirring, not of trains, well-houses,
or tired machines, but the heavy-tread trample of wildflowers
    thundering the pasture of the wild heart.
& When I saw this, I saw wild horses.

J. P. GRASSER

Windchime Meadows—Spring

The first dry weekend in December
Our shearer calls by
Saluting the spring air
Clippers at the ready
Blades oiled and sharpened
Shearing table trestled
Llamas and alpacas marshalled
The shed commandeered
A division of labourers—family and friends
Corrals the woolly herd

The first alpaca
Frothing green spittle at the mouth
A trail of reluctance dragged into the dirt
Is tightly trussed
A rising moan of imagined woe
Drowning the electric buzz
At each shear stroke
Young Tarin gently strokes her neck
Cupping his hand to ruffle her head
Mum, to planned avail
Grasps in turn each hoof
To clip, grout, file and mend
The doctor, Andrew, plays vet
Injecting this year's medicinal
The needle pricks
A camelid wails
The shorn and kempt
Now leaking at all three ends

The chirocatharophiles—those lovers of clean hands
Keep an intended safe distance
Ignoring the commotion
Muck in to sort and grade
Discarding the prickly guard hair
Weeding out soiled fibre
Bagging premium fleece with care
Resisting the childlike urge
To gheegle the unshorn stud
Waiting his turn in the pen

By mid-afternoon, the last of twenty-odd done
A glass of wine deservedly in hand, to drink in the spring sun

ASHLEY CHAN

You Have to Love Them Enough to Let Them be Wild

That's what Steve said
    about the mustangs
        up on Pryor Mountain—

no sugar cubes, no carrots
    no coaxing, stroking, gentling
        no whispering

no ropes, no tires, no pick up trucks
    no dust storm swing low choppers
        no Judas horse

no gathering, no holding pens
    no PZP, no freeze brand
        no breaking in, no putting down

no auction block, no slaughterhouse
    no flank strap, no fast track
        no stockyard, no consignment

no snaffles, bridles, saddles, spurs
    no blankets, shoes, or blinders
        no rodeo, no latigo, no cincha

no clipping, combing, currying
    no conchos, braids or bells
        no ranches, no reata

no binder twine for breech births
    no ligatures, no doctoring
        of tears & rends & bites

no vaccination, no inoculation
        no sterilization
                no intervention

just bales & bales
        of air
                seep water, galleta grass

the animal vegetable mineral
        earth
                exacting, punishing, available

KATHLEEN MCCRACKEN

25 November 2016

It is morning, you look past me to the windows,
and your eyes fill with light,
your eyelashes are jewels, reflections of your inner beauty.
And I—I have the strength to not for another instant
turn my gaze away from you.

MARGARITA SERAFIMOVA

Notes on Contributors

Marsha Barber's two recent poetry books, *What is the Sound of Someone Unravelling* and *All the Lovely Broken People* were published by Ottawa's Borealis Press. She's won many awards for her work and been long-listed for the national ReLit award and short-listed for the international Bridport Poetry Prize. Marsha has published in such periodicals as the *Literary Review of Canada*, *The Walrus*, *FreeFall Magazine* and *The Antigonish Review*. She's on faculty at Ryerson University in Toronto.

Dominique Bernier-Cormier's poetry won The Fiddlehead's 26th Ralph Gustafson Prize, and was shortlisted in Arc Poetry Magazine's Poem of the Year Contest in 2017. His first chapbook, *Englishing*, was recently published by Frog Hollow Press, and his first full-length book of poetry, *Correspondent*, is forthcoming from icehouse (Goose Lane Editions). He is a poetry editor for Rahila's Ghost Press.

Danielle Boodoo-Fortuné is a Trinidadian poet and visual artist. Her work has been featured in the *Small Axe Journal*, *Room Magazine*, *Cordite Poetry Review*, *The Literary Review* and *Poetry London*, as well as in the anthology *Coming Up Hot: Eight New Poets from the Caribbean*. She is the 2012 winner of the Small Axe Poetry Prize, 2015 winner of the Hollick-Arvon Caribbean Writers' Prize and the 2016 winner of the Wasafari New Writing Prize.

Allen Braden is the author of *A Wreath of Down and Drops of Blood* and *Elegy in the Passive Voice*. He was the last generation to grow alfalfa, wheat, barley and cattle on his family's farm of two hundred-plus acres outside White Swan, Washington, on the Yakama Indian Reservation. Assistant Poetry Editor of *Terrain.org: A Journal of the Built + Natural Environment*, he lives in Lakewood, Washington.

Chad Campbell's first collection of poetry *Laws & Locks* (Signal Editions 2015) was shortlisted for the Gerald Lampert Memorial Award. His poetry has appeared in *Brick*, *The Walrus*, and *Best Canadian Poetry*, among others, and a chapbook of recent work *Euphonia* was published earlier this year by Anstruther Press. Chad is a graduate of the Iowa Writers' Workshop and a PhD candidate at the University of Manchester's Centre for New Writing.

Ashley Chan is a composer and poet in his early 40s. He was born and raised in New Zealand and graduated with honours in economics from Auckland University. Inspiration for his work comes from the cosmopolitan city life and the lush rolling hills and golden beaches of the north Auckland countryside. Since 2013, Ashley has been living, working and writing poems in Perth, Western Australia but makes frequent trips back to New Zealand to visit family.

B. R. Dionysius was founding Director of the Queensland Poetry Festival. He has published over 500 poems in literary journals, anthologies, newspapers and online. His eighth poetry collection, *Weranga* was released in 2013. He teaches English at Ipswich Grammar School and lives in Riverhills, Brisbane.

Ann Gamsa came to Montreal from Sweden at the age of 6 ½. She wrote her first poem at age 8, when she was home, sick with the mumps. Since then, she has written many poems, short stories, and stories for her grandchildren. In addition, she has written and published professional articles in her capacity as a psychologist and pain specialist. Writing, various creative projects (e.g. "Honouring Feet"), and acting are amongst her favourite pastimes.

A Wallace Stegner Fellow at Stanford University, **J.P. Grasser** is a PhD candidate in Literature and Creative Writing at the University of Utah, where he edits *Quarterly West*. Previously published work can be found in *32 Poems*, *AGNI*, *Best New Poets 2015*, *Ecotone*, and *West Branch Wired*, among others. For more information, visit www.jpgrasser.com.

James Greene, born in Berlin, has translated Osip Mandelshtam (Penguin, 1991) and, *Love of Beginnings*, the autobiography of J.-B. Pontalis (Free Association Books, 1993); he's also written a tragic comedy about Stalin, *Killing time in the Kremlin* (not yet performed). He has devised scripts for BBC Radio and worked as a gardener in a cemetery and as a psychoanalytic therapist.

Barbara Hobbie, an American, lives in the former East German city of Leipzig and has worked as an independent journalist/essayist, frequently addressing themes of migration and integration. Her poems have appeared in *The Anthology of New England Writers*, *Avant Garde*, *Poetry in Windows*, *Chicago Journalism Review*, *Leipzig Zeitgeist*, *The Granite Review*, and the *Global Poetry Anthology 2011* (Signal Editions).

Rebecca Gayle Howell is the author of *American Purgatory*, selected by Don Share for the 2016 Sexton Prize, and *Render/An Apocalypse*, a finalist for

Foreword Review's 2014 Book of the Year. Among her honors are fellowships from the Fine Arts Work Center and the Carson McCullers Center, as well as a Pushcart Prize. Howell lives in Knott County, Kentucky, where she serves as James Still Writer-in-Residence at the Hindman Settlement School.

Cynthia Hughes writes poetry and music from her home in Southern Vermont, where she is a primary school librarian and teacher. Her poems have been published in several literary journals in the U.S. and have received recognition from poetry awards in the U.S., Ireland and Canada. She is working on her MFA and a first collection of poems.

Wordsmith, craftsperson, teacher, wanderer: life has taken **Jnanama Ishaya** down many paths since she was born in Quebec City, Canada, sixty-three years ago. She's been a farmer and a monk, taught meditation classes around the world, and been a classroom teacher, too. Now a school librarian in a tiny town in BC, she is a little more free to write, make handcrafts, and spend time with her three wonderful dogs and two cats.

Richard James has a B.S. degree in English Lit and a teaching degree. He has, however, made his career in medicine as a Physician's Assistant. He is presently sending out a novel to agents for publication. And he also has a collection of sixteen short stories, and a second novel already written as well as several books of poetry.

Fawzia Muradali Kane was born in San Fernando, Trinidad & Tobago, and practices as an architect in London. Her first collection of poetry *Tantie Diablesse* (Waterloo Press, 2011) was a poetry longlistee for the 2012 Bocas Lit Fest Prize. A long sequence of poems *Houses of the Dead* was published as a pamphlet by Thamesis in 2014. She is currently working on a novel titled *La Bonita Cuentista*.

Maithreyi Karnoor was born in Hubli, India. Her poems, translations, and reviews have been published in national literary journals and publications such as *Indian Literature*, *Muse India*, *The Hindu*, and as part of an anthology by HarperCollins. She is currently translating a Kannada novel into English and is putting together her first collection of poetry. She has an MA in Literary and Cultural Studies. She lives in Goa.

Christopher (Kit) Kelen is a well known Australian poet and painter and Professor of English at the University of Macau, in south China, where he has taught Creative Writing and Literature for the last seventeen years. The most recent of Kelen's fourteen poetry books are *Scavengers' Season* and *A Pocket Kit*. Translated volumes of Kelen's poetry have been published in French, Italian, Spanish, Portuguese, Swedish, Chinese, Filipino and Indonesian.

S. K. Kelen is an Australian poet currently living in the bush capital, enjoys hanging around the house philosophically and travelling. Since winning the Poetry Australia Prize for Poets under 18 in 1973, his works have been widely published in journals, newspapers, and anthologies. Kelen's oeuvre includes pastorals, satires, sonnets, odes, narratives, haiku, epics, idylls, horror stories, sci-fi, allegories, prophecies, politics, history, love poems, portraits, travel poems, memory, people and places, meditations and ecstasies.

Lawrence Kessenich won the 2010 Strokestown International Poetry Prize. His poetry has been published in *Sewanee Review*, *Atlanta Review*, *Poetry Ireland Review* and elsewhere. He has a chapbook, *Strange News*, and two full-length poetry books, *Before Whose Glory* and *Age of Wonders*. Three of his poems were nominated for Pushcart Prizes and three read on Writer's Almanac. Kessenich has also published essays, short plays, short stories and a novel, *Cinnamon Girl*. His website is www.lawrence-writer.com.

Anthony Lawrence's most recent book is *Headwaters* (Pitt Street Poetry, 2016). His books and individual poems have won many of Australia's major awards. He is a Senior lecturer at Griffith University, Gold Coast, where he teaches Creative Writing and Writing Poetry.

Aimee Mackovic is a professor of English and poet living in Austin, TX. Her first full-length poetry collection, *Love Junky*, will be available as of November 2017 from Lit City Press in Austin, TX. Her two chapbooks, *Potpourri* and *Dearly Beloved: the Prince poems*, can be ordered at aimeemackovic.com.

Marjorie Main was born in 1994 and grew up in Torbay, Australia. She currently lives in Melbourne, where she is completing her Honours at the University of Melbourne and putting together a poetry manuscript.

Kathleen McCracken is the author of eight collections of poetry including *Blue Light, Bay and College* (Penumbra Press, 1991), which was shortlisted for the Governor General's Award for Poetry, *A Geography of Souls* (Thistledown Press, 2002), *Mooncalves* (Exile Editions, 2007) and *Tattoo Land* (Exile Editions, 2009). Most recently, a bilingual English/Portuguese edition of her poetry entitled *Double Self Portrait with Mirror: New and Selected Poems*, was published by the Brazilian press, Editora Ex Machina.

Una McDonnell has recited her work at readings and music festivals, and on one occasion, in a boxing ring (Jill Battson's Fighting Words Series). She holds an MFA in Creative Writing from UBC. Her work has appeared in *Arc*, *The New Quarterly*, *Ottawater*, *Prairie Fire*, *Rampike*, and *Musings: An Anthology of Greek-Canadian Literature,* and has been on the longlist for Prism International's Pacific Spirit Poetry Prize, and twice for the CBC Literary Awards.

Amber McMillan is the author of *The Woods: A Year on Protection Island* (2016) and the poetry collection *We Can't Ever Do This Again* (2015). Her work has appeared in *Arc Poetry Magazine*, *PRISM international*, *Best Canadian Poetry*, *The Walrus* and others across North America. She lives and works on BC's Sunshine Coast.

Bruce Meyer is author of more than 60 books of poetry, short fiction, non-fiction, and literary journalism. He won the Gwendolyn MacEwen Prizes in 2015 and 2016. His most recent books of poetry are the award-winning *The Seasons*, *The Arrow of Time*, and *1967: Centennial Year*.

Mary B. Moore's second full-length collection, *Flicker*, won the Dogfish Head Award (judges, Carol Frost, Baron Wormser, and Jan Beatty), and the chapbook *Eating the Light,* won the Sable Books Award (judge, Allison Joseph): both appeared in 2016. Cleveland State published *The Book of Snow* (1998). *Georgia Review*, *Poem/Memoir/Story*, *Cider Press Review*, *Drunken Boat*, *Birmingham Poetry Review* published recent poems. She won *Nimrod's* 2017 Pablo Neruda Contest's Second Place Award.

Anna Murchison hails from Tasmania, a wild, anarchically situated island (see: bottom of the world) inspiring a rich literary tradition. Anna started writing poetry as a means of not losing her mind while working on her first novel. People tell her this has proved only partly successful. Anna finds herself responding to the prevailing noise of narcissism and self-interest by thematically deep-rooting her work in the messy subsoil of life while stubbornly seeking its light.

Peter Norman has published three poetry collections, most recently *The Gun That Starts the Race* (2015), and a novel, *Emberton* (2014). He lives in Toronto. Read more at peternorman.ca.

Felicity Plunkett is the author of *Vanishing Point* (UQP, 2009), *Seastrands* (Vagabond, 2011) and the editor of *Thirty Australian Poets* (UQP, 2011). Her new collection is forthcoming with Pitt St Poetry. She is an Australian poet, critic and editor, and Poetry Editor with University of Queensland Press.

Erin Rodoni is the author of *Body, in Good Light* (Sixteen Rivers Press, 2017) and *A Landscape for Loss* (NFSPS Press, 2017), which won the 2016 Stevens Award sponsored by the National Federation of State Poetry Societies. Her poems have been included in *Best New Poets 2014*, nominated for Pushcart Prizes, and honored with awards from AWP and *Ninth Letter*. She lives in the San Rafael, CA, with her husband and two young daughters.

Kate Rogers' poetry collection *Out of Place* debuted in Toronto July 2017. Her poetry is forthcoming in the anthologies *Catherines the Great* (Oolichan) and *Twin Cities Cinema* (Hong Kong-Singapore), and has appeared in *The Guardian*, *Eastlit*, *Asia Literary Review*, *Cha: An Asian Literary Journal*, *Morel*, *The Goose: A Journal of Arts, Environment and Culture* (Wilfred Laurier University), *Kyoto Journal*, *ASIATIC: the Journal of the International Islamic University of Malaysia* and *Contemporary Verse II*.

Linda Rogers, a Victoria Poet Laureate and Canadian People's Poet, mother of four, married to mandolinist Rick van Krugel, writes fiction, song lyrics and literary and social criticism. Her most recent novel is *Bozuk*, a Turkish memoir from Exile Editions. Forthcoming is *Repairing the Hive*, the final book in her Empress Trilogy and *Crow Jazz*, a short story collection from Mother Tongue.

Margarita Serafimova has published two collections in Bulgarian, *Animals and Other Gods* (2016), and *Demons and World* (2017). Her work appears in *London Grip New Poetry*, *Agenda*, *A-Minor*, *Trafika Europe*, *Minor Literatures*, *The Journal*, *Noble / Gas*, *Ink, Sweat and Tears*, *The Birds We Piled Loosely*, *Obra/ Artifact*, *Futures Trading*, *Poetic Diversity*, *TAYO*,

Ginosko, Dark Matter, The Punch, Window Quarterly/ Patient Sounds, Peacock Journal, Anti-Heroin Chic, In Between Hangovers, and elsewhere. For more poetry from Margarita: https://www.facebook.com/MargaritaISerafimova/?ref=aymt_homepage_panel.

Born and raised in Australia, **Chloe Sparks** spent the better part of the last decade living in Vancouver, BC working on various film and television productions and at a local newspaper as a research assistant. She is working towards a Masters Degree in Communications and building a social media presence.

Elizabet Stevens lives where she was born in Southern New Brunswick. Her poem "Homestead" is from a recently-completed collection, *Blue Forensics: a case of heartbreak*. Her work has appeared in literary magazines and received recognition in poetry competitions. She has taken part in readings as far away as Effat University, Jeddah, Saudi Arabia where she was an instructor. A former journalist, Elizabet worked for the CBC, and was a contributor to the *Globe and Mail*.

Derek Sugamosto was born and raised in Southeast Michigan. His work has previously appeared in *apt, Wisconsin Review, Orange Coast Review, Coe Review, Dogwood, Sheepshead Review, Two Thirds North, Dewpoint, Qua, Paper Nautilus* and *Sugar House Review*.

Bruce Van Noy was born in Seattle, raised in North California, educated in genetics and molecular biology at the University of California, Berkley. He studied poetry under Barney Childs at the University of Redlands. A former commercial fisherman in Alaska, and a professional ski instructor based in Ketchum, Idaho, he currently lives on Orcas Island, a few miles off the far north-western coast of Washington, and a stone's throw across the water from Canada.

Zoe VanGunten reads and writes whenever and wherever luck strikes: Toledo, El Rito, Austin, Pamplona, Sevilla, Santa Fe—always on the bus at the last moment and happier nearer a window. This poem was written during a snowy Alamosa winter in the company of two very old German breed dogs and a tall bundled man faceting gemstones in the garage.

Bryan Walpert is the author of three poetry collections—*Etymology, A History of Glass,* and *Native Bird*—as well as the fiction collection *Ephraim's*

Eyes and the scholarly monograph *Resistance to Science in Contemporary American Poetry* (Routledge). A defense of poetry, *Poetry and Mindfulness*, is forthcoming this year. He teaches Creative Writing as an Associate Professor in the School of English & Media Studies at Massey University in Auckland, New Zealand. Learn more at bryanwalpert.com.

Julie Watts is a Western Australian writer and Play Therapist. She has been published in various journals and anthologies including: *Westerly*, *Cordite*, *Australian Poetry Anthology*, *Australian Love Poems 2013* and the *Anthology of Contemporary Australian Feminist Poetry*. In 2016 she won The National Association of Loss and Grief Award and was short listed in the Newcastle Poetry Prize. Her first poetry collection, *Honey and Hemlock*, was published in 2013 by Sunline Press.

Abigail Wieser is a recent graduate from Millikin University in Decateur, IL. She has had poetry appear in various places, including *Stepping Stones Magazine* and Millikin's literary journal, *The Collage*. She is excited to get married this summer, work on her book of poems, and bless the community of Decateur with the River Coffee Company she and her fiancé are starting this fall.

Karey Willan has been stringing words together for much of her adult life, either through working as a verbatim shorthand reporter or chasing to light a skittish muse. Karey's fascination with psychology propels her art. She is an adventurist of the mind and BC's mountainous terrain. Karey holds a BFA (with distinction) from UVic in Visual Arts and a professional writing diploma from Douglas College, where she was a summer intern for *Event Magazine*.

Lauren Williams was born and raised in Melbourne, Australia; she now resides in the historic country town of Maldon, central Victoria. She began writing poetry in the early 1980s, and has performed widely, nationally and internationally. Lauren's sixth collection, *Cleanskin Poems*, was published by Island Press (Sydney) in 2016. She is also a prize-winning singer/songwriter.

David Mark Williams lives in south west Scotland. He is widely published in magazines and anthologies and has won prizes for his poetry in the UK and New Zealand. His first full-length collection of poetry, *The Odd Sock Exchange*, was published by Cinnamon Press in 2015.

Catriona Wright is the author of *Table Manners* (Véhicule Press, 2017). Her poems have appeared in *Prism International, Prairie Fire, Rusty Toque, Lemon Hound, The Best Canadian Poetry 2015,* and elsewhere.

Notes on Editors

Kim Addonizio is the author of six poetry collections, two novels, two story collections, and two books on writing poetry. She has received fellowships from the NEA and Guggenheim Foundations, two Pushcart Prizes, and was a National Book Award Finalist.

David Dabydeen has won the Quiller-Couch English Prize and the Commonwealth Poetry Prize. He is a professor at the University of Warwick, and Guyana's Ambassador for UNESCO. He is a Fellow of the Royal Society of Literature and has received many awards including the Hind Rattan Award and the Anthony N. Sabga award.

Vona Groarke is the author of seven collections of poetry. Her poems have appeared in *The New Yorker, The Guardian, Poetry* and many more. She teaches at the University of Manchester and is the editor of Poetry Ireland Review and selector for the Poetry Book Society (U.K.).

Susan Nalugwa Kiguli is an academic and poet. She was the African Studies Association Presidential Fellow 2011. She has served as the chairperson of Uganda Women Writers' Association, and she currently serves on the Advisory Board for the African Writers Trust.

Arvind Krishna Mehrotra has published five books of poems, and two of translation. Among the books he has edited are the *Oxford India Anthology of Twelve Modern Indian Poets* and *A History of Indian Literature in English*. He lives in Dehradun, India.

Pascale Petit is the author of six collections of poetry. She won the Manchester Poetry Prize and was shortlisted for the Wales Book of the Year and four times for the T. S. Eliot Prize. As well, she is the recipient of a Cholmondeley Award. She lives in the UK.

Talya Rubin is a writer and performance maker. Her poetry won the Bronwen Wallace Award for Emerging Writers and was short-listed for the Winston Collins/Descant prize for Best Canadian poem and the Montreal International Poetry Prize. She runs an interdisciplinary performance company and currently lives in Montreal.

Carmine Starnino is the author of five volumes of poetry and two collections of literary essays. His work was nominated for a Governor General's Award and the Pushcart Prize. He is the poetry editor at Véhicule Press and senior editor at Walrus Magazine. He lives in Toronto.

Mark Tredinnick is a poet, nature writer, writing teacher, and memoirist. Winner of the 2011 Montreal Poetry Prize, and of the 2011 Cardiff Poetry Prize, he is currently the poet in residence at the Sydney Botanic Gardens. He lives and writes along the Wingecarribee River, southwest of Sydney.

Joseph Akawu Ushie is a Fellow of the 2002 Fulbright Program and his State Government's Honouree for outstanding contributions to the growth of African Literature and Culture. His poetry has been widely anthologized. He lectures at the University of Uyo, Nigeria and has been a Visiting Lecturer at the Niger Delta University and at the Omar Bongo University, Gabon.

Author Index

Marsha Barber 27
Dominique Bernier-Cormier 17
Danielle Boodoo-Fortuné 20
Allen Braden 33
Chad Campbell 13
Ashley Chan 82
Brett Dionysius 31
Ann Gamsa 36
J. P. Grasser 81
James Greene 23
Barbara Hobbie 29
Rebecca Gayle Howell 76
Cynthia Hughes 74, 80
Jnanama Ishaya 38
Richard James 52
Fawzia Muradali Kane 40
Maithreyi Karnoor 24
Christopher (Kit) Kelen 15, 72
S. K. Kelen 58
Lawrence Kessenich 25
Anthony Lawrence 18
Aimee Mackovic 78
Marjorie Main 70
Kathleen McCracken 84
Una McDonnell 46
Amber McMillan 48
Bruce Meyer 56, 57
Mary B. Moore 16
Anna Murchison 63
Peter Norman 65
Felicity Plunkett 67
Erin Rodoni 21
Kate Rogers 44
Linda Rogers 22
Margarita Serafimova 86
Chloe Sparks 47
Elizabet Stevens 35

Derek Sugamosto 68
Bruce Van Noy 71
Zoe VanGunten 60
Bryan Walpert 75
Julie Watts 11
Abigail Wieser 61
Karey Willan 49
Lauren Williams 42
David Mark Williams 51
Catriona Wright 54

Carmine Starnino, Editor
Michael Harris, Founding Editor

SELECTED POEMS David Solway
THE MULBERRY MEN David Solway
A SLOW LIGHT Ross Leckie
NIGHT LETTERS Bill Furey
COMPLICITY Susan Glickman
A NUN'S DIARY Ann Diamond
CAVALIER IN A ROUNDHEAD SCHOOL Errol MacDonald
VEILED COUNTRIES/LIVES Marie-Claire Blais (Translated by Michael Harris)
BLIND PAINTING Robert Melançon (Translated by Philip Stratford)
SMALL HORSES & INTIMATE BEASTS Michel Garneau
 (Translated by Robert McGee)
IN TRANSIT Michael Harris
THE FABULOUS DISGUISE OF OURSELVES Jan Conn
ASHBOURN John Reibetanz
THE POWER TO MOVE Susan Glickman
MAGELLAN'S CLOUDS Robert Allen
MODERN MARRIAGE David Solway
K. IN LOVE Don Coles
THE INVISIBLE MOON Carla Hartsfield
ALONG THE ROAD FROM EDEN George Ellenbogen
DUNINO Stephen Scobie
KINETIC MUSTACHE Arthur Clark
RUE SAINTE FAMILLE Charlotte Hussey
HENRY MOORE'S SHEEP Susan Glickman
SOUTH OF THE TUDO BEM CAFÉ Jan Conn
THE INVENTION OF HONEY Ricardo Sternberg
EVENINGS AT LOOSE ENDS Gérald Godin (Translated by Judith Cowan)
THE PROVING GROUNDS Rhea Tregebov
LITTLE BIRD Don Coles
HOMETOWN Laura Lush
FORTRESS OF CHAIRS Elisabeth Harvor
NEW & SELECTED POEMS Michael Harris
BEDROCK David Solway
TERRORIST LETTERS Ann Diamond
THE SIGNAL ANTHOLOGY Edited by Michael Harris
MURMUR OF THE STARS: SELECTED SHORTER POEMS Peter Dale Scott
WHAT DANTE DID WITH LOSS Jan Conn
MORNING WATCH John Reibetanz
JOY IS NOT MY PROFESSION Muhammad al-Maghut
 (Translated by John Asfour and Alison Burch)
WRESTLING WITH ANGELS: SELECTED POEMS Doug Beardsley
HIDE & SEEK Susan Glickman
MAPPING THE CHAOS Rhea Tregebov
FIRE NEVER SLEEPS Carla Hartsfield
THE RHINO GATE POEMS George Ellenbogen
SHADOW CABINET Richard Sanger
MAP OF DREAMS Ricardo Sternberg
THE NEW WORLD Carmine Starnino
THE LONG COLD GREEN EVENINGS OF SPRING Elisabeth Harvor
KEEP IT ALL Yves Boisvert (Translated by Judith Cowan)

THE GREEN ALEMBIC Louise Fabiani
THE ISLAND IN WINTER Terence Young
A TINKERS' PICNIC Peter Richardson
SARACEN ISLAND: THE POEMS OF ANDREAS KARAVIS David Solway
BEAUTIES ON MAD RIVER: SELECTED AND NEW POEMS Jan Conn
WIND AND ROOT Brent MacLaine
HISTORIES Andrew Steinmetz
ARABY Eric Ormsby
WORDS THAT WALK IN THE NIGHT Pierre Morency
  (Translated by Lissa Cowan and René Brisebois)
A PICNIC ON ICE: SELECTED POEMS Matthew Sweeney
HELIX: NEW AND SELECTED POEMS John Steffler
HERESIES: THE COMPLETE POEMS OF ANNE WILKINSON, 1924-1961
  Edited by Dean Irvine
CALLING HOME Richard Sanger
FIELDER'S CHOICE Elise Partridge
MERRYBEGOT Mary Dalton
MOUNTAIN TEA Peter Van Toorn
AN ABC OF BELLY WORK Peter Richardson
RUNNING IN PROSPECT CEMETERY Susan Glickman
MIRABEL Pierre Nepveu (Translated by Judith Cowan)
POSTSCRIPT Geoffrey Cook
STANDING WAVE Robert Allen
THERE, THERE Patrick Warner
HOW WE ALL SWIFTLY: THE FIRST SIX BOOKS Don Coles
THE NEW CANON: AN ANTHOLOGY OF CANADIAN POETRY
  Edited by Carmine Starnino
OUT TO DRY IN CAPE BRETON Anita Lahey
RED LEDGER Mary Dalton
REACHING FOR CLEAR David Solway
OX Christopher Patton
THE MECHANICAL BIRD Asa Boxer
SYMPATHY FOR THE COURIERS Peter Richardson
MORNING GOTHIC: NEW AND SELECTED POEMS George Ellenbogen
36 CORNELIAN AVENUE Christopher Wiseman
THE EMPIRE'S MISSING LINKS Walid Bitar
PENNY DREADFUL Shannon Stewart
THE STREAM EXPOSED WITH ALL ITS STONES D.G. Jones
PURE PRODUCT Jason Guriel
ANIMALS OF MY OWN KIND Harry Thurston
BOXING THE COMPASS Richard Greene
CIRCUS Michael Harris
THE CROW'S VOW Susan Briscoe
WHERE WE MIGHT HAVE BEEN Don Coles
MERIDIAN LINE Paul Bélanger (Translated by Judith Cowan)
SKULLDUGGERY Asa Boxer
SPINNING SIDE KICK Anita Lahey
THE ID KID Linda Besner
GIFT HORSE Mark Callanan
SUMPTUARY LAWS Nyla Matuk
THE GOLDEN BOOK OF BOVINITIES Robert Moore
MAJOR VERBS Pierre Nepveu (Translated by Donald Winkler)
ALL SOULS' Rhea Tregebov
THE SMOOTH YARROW Susan Glickman
THE GREY TOTE Deena Kara Shaffer
HOOKING Mary Dalton

DANTE'S HOUSE Richard Greene
BIRDS FLOCK FISH SCHOOL Edward Carson
SATISFYING CLICKING SOUND Jason Guriel
DOG EAR Jim Johnstone
THE SCARBOROUGH Michael Lista
RADIO WEATHER Shoshanna Wingate
LAWS & LOCKS Chad Campbell
LEAVING THE ISLAND Talya Rubin
INSTALLATIONS David Solway
MOCKINGBIRD Derek Webster
LATE VICTORIANS Vincent Colistro
MODEL DISCIPLE Michael Prior
BASED ON ACTUAL EVENTS Robert Moore
STRANGER Nyla Matuk
SIREN Kateri Lanthier
TABLE MANNERS Catriona Wright
SHIP OF GOLD: THE ESSENTIAL POEMS OF ÉMILE NELLIGAN (Trans. by Marc di Saverio)
THE CHEMICAL LIFE Jim Johnstone
GLOBAL POETRY ANTHOLOGY 2017 Edited by Kim Addonizio, David Dabydeen & others